THE COURT
OF
ELIZABETH THE FIRST

THE COURT
OF
ELIZABETH THE FIRST

by

Rachel and Allen Percival

STAINER AND BELL

82 HIGH ROAD

LONDON N2 9PW

First Published in 1976
by Stainer and Bell Limited
82 High Road, London N2 9PW

Printed in Great Britain
by Galliard (Printers) Limited, Great Yarmouth

SBN 85249 279 0

CONTENTS

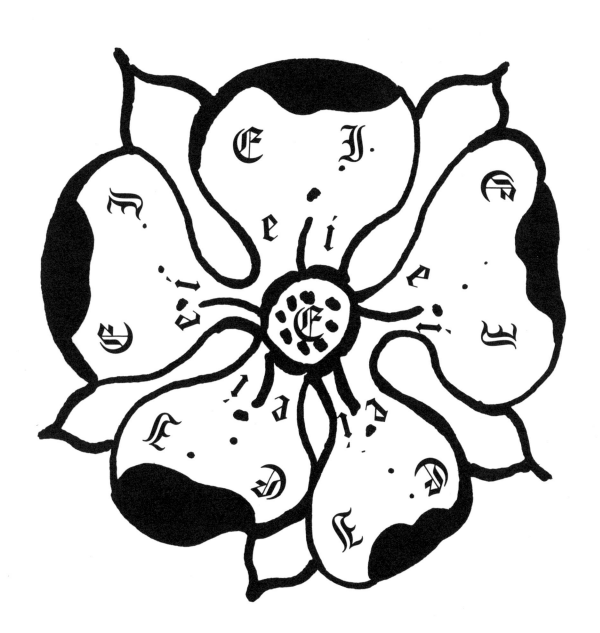

6

PREFACE

Amongst the vast amount written on Elizabethan England, comparatively little attention has been given to the part played by the performing arts in everyday life. This short, illustrated history of Elizabeth's reign is told through a series of 'episodes' which attempt to describe not only events but what those events looked and sounded like.

So the reader will find maps, drawings, facsimiles and music which combine with the story to give as accurate a 'sound picture' of Elizabethan society as we have been able to piece together. With accounts of dancing in court and country, dress and costume, music in church, palace and country house, staging of plays, popular music at a feast, a hunt and in the street— alongside portraits of those who made the Court of Elizabeth the envy of Europe and pictures of some of the places where they lived—we hope we have added an interesting postscript to the social history of England.

Sources of all illustrations, drawings, musical extracts and evidence on which to base the presentation of Elizabethan plays, music and 'entertainments' are given so that a reader may put this information to practical use in school or college, house or church. With all the books about, and editions of, Elizabethan plays and music now available, no one need produce 'Tudor-type' sets, costumes or incidental music. By aiming at authentic re-construction—even though using modern instruments and materials—those interested in social history may see it in a new light themselves and, perhaps, enlighten others.

We are most grateful to Peter Bucknell for making his wide knowledge of Elizabethan theatre and costume so freely available to us, and to Leslie East and William Oxenbury for their help in collecting material for reproduction.

Cambridge 1976   Rachel and Allen Percival

THE ILLUSTRATIONS

THE ILLUSTRATIONS

ACKNOWLEDGMENTS

The authors are grateful to the following for permission to reproduce photographs of woodcuts, drawings, paintings, manuscripts and buildings in their care:

The Controller of Her Majesty's Stationery Office	pages 22, 42, 43, 46
The Dean and Canons of Windsor	33
The Dean and Chapter of Westminster	19, 20
The Trustees of the British Museum	12, 16, 18, 20, 22, 30, 33, 35, 38, 44, 60, 78, 91, 98, 99
The Trustees of the National Portrait Gallery	24, 41, 67, 69, 77, 80, 81, 83, 84
The Trustees of Dulwich Gallery	81
University of London Library	74
University of Oxford Faculty of Music	96
The Master of the Temple	25
Michael Ward Thomas, Esq.	57
The Reverend G. R. Phizackerly, St Faith's Church, King's Lynn	71
Lord Brooke of Warwick Castle	21

THE EPISODES

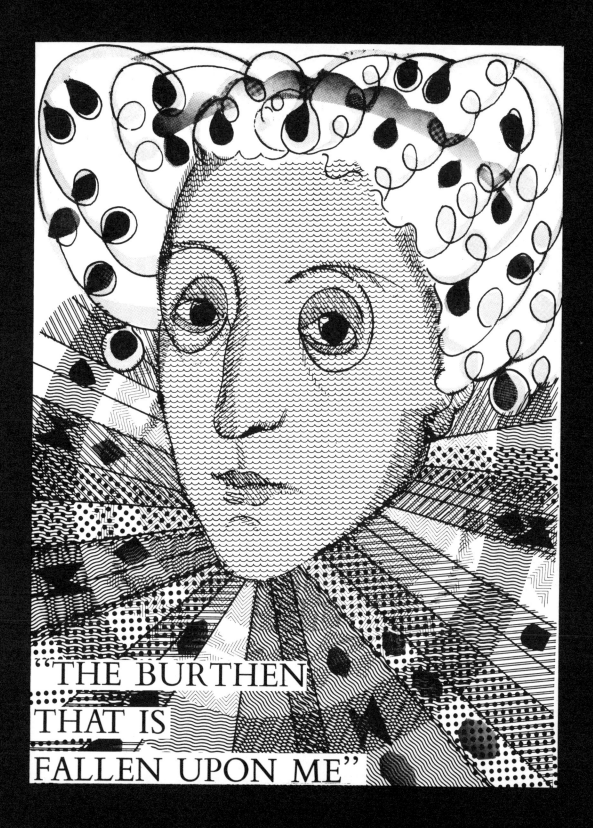

"THE BURTHEN THAT IS FALLEN UPON ME"

ELIZABETH Tudor entered London on November the 28th, 1558, proclaimed Queen of England. She was 25 and, as she herself said, 'mere English' as she was descended from Kings of England on the one side and a Lord Mayor of London on the other. The citizens of London welcomed her with great joy . . . and music.

At Shoreditch, even before she entered the City gate on her journey from Hatfield House, she paused to listen to the famous bells. The following day when she took possession of the Tower of London the noise from Barbican to Bishopsgate and Tower Hill was continuous; but the most impressive welcome of all was reserved for the procession from the Tower to Westminster on the eve of her Coronation, January the 14th, 1559.

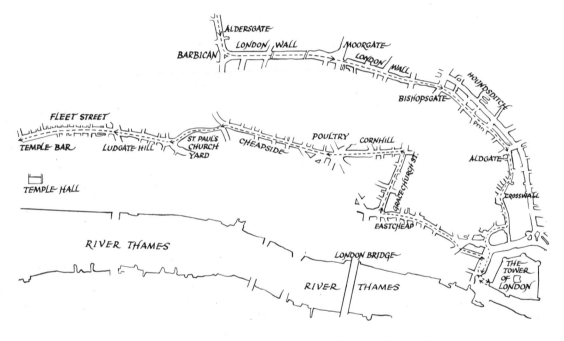

The routes followed by Elizabeth from Aldersgate to the Tower, and from the Tower to Temple Bar in 1558/9, as they still are today.

As with today's Lord Mayor's Show, it was a Saturday. All along the route pageants had been prepared. Loud instruments played in Gracechurch Street, soft instruments made 'heavenlie melodie' in Cornhill. By St. Peter's in Cheapside the Waits had their traditional stand, beyond the Lord Mayor's trumpeters. The children of St. Paul's sang outside their school. At the Lord's Gate (Ludgate) minstrels brayed on their loud instruments as the young Queen crossed the river Fleet. More children sang at Temple Bar where she bade farewell to the Lord Mayor and Sheriffs and so to the City of London.

The Waits were the 'official' musicians, wore the servant's blue coat but with sleeves in the City's colours of red and white, and proudly carried a badge of the City's arms on their long silver chains.

In 1553, the Waits probably only had these instruments between them, according to the minutes of The Court of Common Council which governed, and still governs, the City of London:

LOUD
- Trumpets
- Shawms (Oboe, Bassoon)
- Sackbuts (Trombone)
- Fife (Piccolo)
- Drums and Cymbals

SOFT
- Lute (Guitar)
- Flutes (Recorders)

Instruments named in parentheses are possible modern substitutes.

There were only six City Waits in 1558 and they would have taken up their traditional place in Cheapside. The Fellowship of Minstrels, together with the Fellowship of Parish Clerks, must have played and sung at various places from little tapestry-hung stages; the Minstrels were also complaining bitterly at the time about competition from outsiders and 'foreigners' in the City. The eye-witness who lodged his account of the procession at Stationer's Hall within days of the event most probably only mentioned the music he particularly remembered. In fact the noise—not all of it musical—including every church bell along the route must have been a fair test of Elizabeth's endurance. Even on a quiet Sunday morning it takes two hours to walk from Bishopsgate to Temple Bar at the slow speed of a procession.

This old French tune was a favourite of Henry VIII and would have been well known to
the Waits and minstrels. It can be played on any combination of 'loud' instruments in
the list on page 15, drum and cymbals adding the rhythm 'long, short-short' to each
bar as in the first bar of the tune.

The Lord Mayor of London, two Common
Councilmen, the Dean of St. Paul's with the
Lord Mayor's Chaplain, and four State
Trumpeters.

"GOD'S CREATURE"

ONCE outside the City, the procession continued at the back of the riverside houses (the 'Strand'), past Charing Cross (that is, 'Turning Cross' where there is a bend in the Thames), coming at last to the Queen's Palace in Whitehall.

The Courtyard of the Palace in Whitehall, with Westminster Abbey overlooking the left, according to an early 17th-century etching.

The following morning, Sunday January the 15th, 1559, the Earls of Shrewsbury and Pembroke presented 'God's creature' to the church and peers of the realm in Westminster Abbey. Escorted by halberdiers she arrived to the inevitable fanfares and bellringing. On her entrance she was received by the Choir with the anthem "Let thy hand be strengthened" in Latin, beginning *Firmetur*; before the anointing came *Unxerunt Salomonem*, known to us as "Zadok the Priest"; and, before the Crowning, *Confortare* ("Be strong and play the man"). The last two anthems have been sung in different settings at all four coronations in this century.

In the order of homage before the crowning, Elizabeth made a significant change: instead of Bishop, Clergy and Peers, she decreed Bishop, Peers and Clergy—the State before the Church.

A few weeks before the Coronation the Lord Mayor of London (who took precedence over all other 'peers') had ordered that the Epistle and Gospel should be read in English at mass in the City of London. In the oath of allegiance which all had to swear at the Coronation, the Sovereign was named "Supreme Head of the Church". As none of Roman faith could accept this there must have been many troubled consciences when the young Queen mounted the tribune between the High Altar and the Choir to receive their homage.

Photo. Nicholas Servian, Woodmansterne Limited

The Choir and High Altar of Westminster Abbey today.

The Coronation Chair in Westminster Abbey.

The mass was to be that normally ordained for that Sunday. The introduction, however, was traditional to the Coronation. *Protector Noster* was started by the Dean as it had been at the coronations of Henry VII and Henry VIII and the Bishop of Carlisle (the 70-year old Oglethorpe) began in Latin.

But the quality of Elizabeth's diplomacy was soon to be seen. The Gospel was read first in Latin, then repeated in English and both the Lord's Prayer and the Bidding Prayer were spoken in English. After these, as she herself could not accept the ceremony of the elevation of the Host, the Queen withdrew into a side chapel and did not take Communion.

Part of the Coronation Procession as an eye-witness remembered it.

The places of State and Church became even clearer as the procession left the Abbey. Her Majesty's Chapel—Dean, Sub-Dean, seven priests, twenty-six choirmen, the Master of the Children and his twelve Choirboys and the six vestrymen—came last.

The 'Coronation' portrait. Reproduced by kind permission of Lord Brooke of Warwick
Castle.

THE Queen, having shown that the State took precedence over the Church, had to be sure of the lawyers. Then, as now, the Temple—between Temple Bar and the river Thames—was the centre of legal training and there, every Christmas, the celebrations were by custom presided over by a royal representative nominated as 'Constable and Marshal' specially for the festivities by the monarch.

In 1561 the Queen went to the Twelfth Night celebrations which included a play. The gentlemen of the Temple chose a play called *Gorboduc* which relates a legendary tale of early English quarrels over the succession to the throne and the destruction of the country through civil war. Perhaps Elizabeth, always sensitive to the suggestion of her cousin Mary as a rival claimant to the throne of England, heard more than the gentlemen-actors intended. At all events, the nominated Marshal for the following year was her favourite, Lord Robert Dudley, who could in her estimation be sure to bring back exact assessments of the loyalty of the Temple.

Lord Robert Dudley. Although he was 'Sweet Robin' for most of his life to Elizabeth, the Earl of Sussex felt very differently about this violent, handsome and unpredictable courtier. "Beware of the gipsy!" he told his friends, "You know not the beast as well as I do".

The Christmas 'Revels' at the Temple lasted from Christmas Eve until Twelfth Night. If banquets loosened tongues then as they often do today, the scale of the Temple feasts must have made Dudley's task easier. The Hall of the Middle Temple was arranged in strict hierarchical order, as it is today:

Magistrates and barristers sat on one side of the table only, facing each other across the hall; the clerks and stewards with their staffs sat on both sides. At High Table sat the Marshal with the chief guests and former Masters of the Revels. The orders for Christmas Eve give a remarkably detailed account of the feast:

"The butlers or Christmas Servants [extra staff] are first to cover the tables with fair linen cloths and furnish the first three highest tables with salt cellars, napkins and trenchers [wooden platters], bread and a silver spoon."

At the other tables the servants were to lay bread only, true to the phrase sometimes still heard of being 'below the salt', meaning low in rank.

"At the first course the minstrels must sound their instruments and go before; and the Steward and Marshal are next to follow together and after them the Gentleman Sewer; and then cometh the meat. The three officers are to make three solemn courtesies [bending the knees] at three several times between the screen and the high table—at the end, middle and top of the Benchers' Table. Then standing by, the Sewer performeth his office."

The Sewer ceremonially served the first portion and the other tables were then served in strict order of precedence:

"All which time the music must stand right above the hearth side with the noise of their music, their faces directed towards the highest table; and that done, to return into the buttery with their music sounding."

The 'music' referred to here were trumpeters, fife and drum sounding what the writer called "the courageous blast of deadly war".

Any 'loud' instruments can play these calls, repeating and varying them at will. In the processional pavan which follows, any group of strings and recorders can recall the sound the writer remembered, with guitar playing the chords shown and a muted trombone playing the bass line to represent a sackbut.

The same writer recalls "the sweet harmony of violins, sackbuts, recorders and cornetts [see page 15] with other instruments of music as it seemed Apollo's harp had tuned their stroke." Vague though he was about detail, there is perhaps enough in his account to imagine that the trumpeters heralded the entry of each course with fife and drum and that the others played a processional pavan until the three highest tables were served.

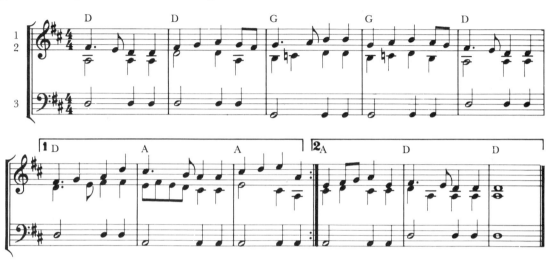

After the second course "the servants and musicians are to resort to the place assigned for them to dine at, which is the Valet's or Yeoman's table beneath the screen. Dinner ended, the musicians sing a song at High Table."

The diners were then to get up and leave. By now it was evidently expected that the food and drink might have taken its effect for in the orders the clerks and stewards were told "to avoid tables in fair and decent manner". They were to leave in order of seniority until the High Table only was left.

The tables were cleared and "after a little repose, the persons at the High Table arise and prepare to revels". The singing and dancing which followed were begun by the oldest Master of the Revels among the guests, who had to begin a carol in which the whole company joined. One, perhaps still the most popular despite its Catholic association, was "Blessed be that Maid Marie". This old dancing carol was based on the same migratory tune as that of the Staines Morris Men and is still to be found in some carol books today.

Over the whole twelve days, various customs were observed. On Christmas Day itself, the musicians sang in the meat course—boar's head—with the carol as we still know it. On St. Stephen's Day (our Boxing Day) dinner had a country theme.

The Marshal and his Lieutenant entered the Hall in full armour with crested helmets, with 16 trumpeters to provide the flourish. To the pavan, they processed three times round the fire before the Lord Chancellor led the Marshal to his seat.

Then came the Master of the Game in green velvet, with the Forest Rangers in green satin carrying green bows and arrows and hunting horn slung round the neck, to a traditional call:

"The Call for the Companie in the Morning."

A huntsman brought in a fox in a net and a cat tied to a staff. At the second signal, a pack of hounds was let loose at the door:

"The Seeke" (when the hounds are let loose).

and to a flurry of horn calls set upon the animals:

"The Rechate" (when the hounds have found the quarry).

The Elizabethans would never have thought what appears cruel to us to be anything else but sport.

This was the beginning of 'the entertainment': the Master of the Game was formally welcomed and the oldest Master of the Revels again began the singing. An obvious choice was the very popular "All in a garden green".

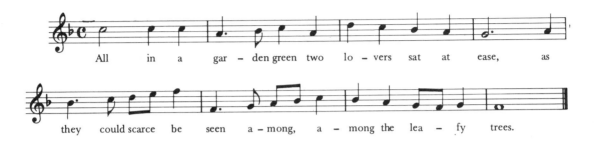

All in a gar - den green two lo - vers sat at ease, as
they could scarce be seen a - mong, a - mong the lea - fy trees.

At the end of the evening, the Marshal was carried on a 'scaffold' chair by four Rangers round the hearth *three times*—again the symbolic figure—with everyone shouting "A Lord, a Lord, a Lord!".

Yeomen and valets. Musicians and servants dining at the same table would wear similar livery.

Some guests remained in the Temple throughout the holiday and some, such as the 'King of the Cockneys' (today's 'Pearly King') came to specific feasts. The night before the twelfth day of Christmas was the climax, for the play and mask. To this were invited all the heads of other legal 'Inns' and Houses of the Courts of Law with their ladies. But after the play, the ladies dined alone in the library whilst the gentlemen of the Temple served their husbands at the Lord Chancellor's Dinner in Hall. When the banquet was over, the Marshal's orders were that he "deviseth some sport for passing away the rest of the night". It was rumoured that Lord Dudley, Marshal for 1562, would be created Earl of Leicester on Twelfth Night. The Queen disappointed the gossips . . . and 'the Gipsy' had to wait a little longer.

HONI
QUI
PENSE

SOIT
MAL Y

31

QUEEN Elizabeth had a passion for dress and was said to have over 2,000 in her wardrobe. She loved large gatherings and noise. The sound of a large choir appealed to her and she seems to have enjoyed the flattery in the many plays written to be acted before her by the boys of the Royal Choir. On the Feast of St. George, all could be indulged in one day, for on April the 23rd every year "The Queen's Majesty's Progenitors, Founders of the most noble Order of the Garter" were (and are still) commemorated at Windsor.

Twenty trumpeters heralded the Queen's arrival. Following a grand procession of the Chapel Royal (30 chaplains in capes of cloth of gold, 43 gowned gentlemen choristers and choirboys in scarlet) and the Knights of the Garter in full robes, Elizabeth entered the Chapel of St. George for the service of Morning Prayer.

The building was perfumed with incense for the occasion and the lessons (Ecclesiasticus 44, "Let us now praise famous men" and John 15, "I am the true Vine") were followed by a special prayer:
"Grant also, O Lord, to the noble society of the most honourable Order of the Garter, Joshua's holiness, David's integrity, Solomon's wisdom and Gideon's good success, in all their services for and under thine anointed Elizabeth our Queen, that so their peaceable practices and martial feats being begun, continued and ended in thee, may be so prospered by thee as still we may wonder at thy mighty works and magnify thy mercy, through Jesus Christ our Lord. Amen."

The Litany began, in Cranmer's translation, "O God, the Father of Heaven":

In this setting by Thomas Tallis the plainsong 'tones' form the top tune. Harmonisation of this kind was undoubtedly meant for the Chapel Royal choir since congregational singing (see page 38) always had the tune in the tenor. The setting ends with the Lord's Prayer.

The Choir of St. George's Chapel, Windsor, 1973, looking west.

Photo. A. C. Cooper Limited

After the service came 'the anthem':

William Byrd wrote the anthem which begins like this, for some special occasion and
the Garter Service seems a likely one . . . but no one can be sure.

34

From 1562 onwards, the ending to St. George's Day was 'The Choirboy's Play'. Choirboys of the Chapel Royal came from all over the country, picked and brought to London by members of the Chapel who travelled wide in search of good voices. Press-gang methods manned the Queen's ships and in perhaps a more peaceable form they provided her choir. The chosen choirboys were, however, all well fed, clothed and educated.

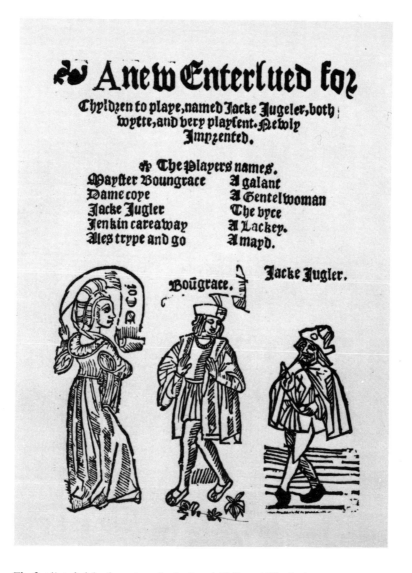

The first 'interlude' to be registered at Stationer's Hall as a children's play, 1562. No music has survived from the earlier Choirboy plays, but the exquisite lullaby which follows on the next pages could well come from a later one with its reference to Troy, since 'classical' plots were very popular. The original viol accompaniment can easily go on three violins and cello (best muted).

SOLO VOICE

My lit – tle sweet dar – ling, my com-fort and

joy. Sing lul – la – by lul – ly.
In beau – ty sur-pas-sing the

prin – ces of Troy. Sing lul – la-by, lul-ly.
Now suck child and

sleep child, thy mo – ther's sweet boy. Sing lul – la-by, lul-ly.
The

36

gods bless and keep thee from cru - el an - noy Sing lul - ly, lul-ly, lul-ly, sweet

ba - by lul-ly, lul - ly sweet ba - by, lul - la - by, lul - ly. -

So, perhaps, ended one St. George's Day at Windsor, in the 1570s.

From 1570 onwards, the anniversary of the Queen's accession had been proclaimed a Protestant 'Holy Day' (holiday) when bells were rung, services sung and bonfires lit after an evening's revels all over the country. (In some country villages this custom went on into the eighteenth century only being ousted finally by the fireworks of Guy Fawkes Night.) By the 1580s, Elizabeth the 'Virgin Queen' was in many simple minds confused with the Virgin Queen of Heaven in the old Roman religion, for a nation accustomed for centuries to the worship of the Virgin could not easily lose its associations.

The Puritans encouraged the country people in this worship of the Queen as a means of destroying the hierarchy of the bishops and it seemed in the early days of her reign that Elizabeth continued to face both ways.

In the Articles of Religion of 1562, she had declared: "It is a thing plainly repugnant to the Word of God . . . to have public prayer in the Church . . . in a tongue not understood of the people". Outside the Chapel Royal, the emphasis was on congregational singing and 'understanding' the service.

John Day, whose publishing house was over the same Alderman's Gate (Aldersgate) by which Elizabeth first entered London as Queen, offered for sale the first psalms put into simple English metre together with 65 tunes in 1563. Two followers of Calvin, the clergymen Sternhold and Hopkins, had made the metrical version of the words 13 years earlier, but Day's book and its tunes were the 'authorized version' for psalms sung in the Church of England until the eighteenth century.

The tunes mostly came from Dutch folk tunes used for the first metrical Psalter at Antwerp in 1539. Day acknowledged this by calling them 'old' tunes with the number of the psalm to which they had belonged.

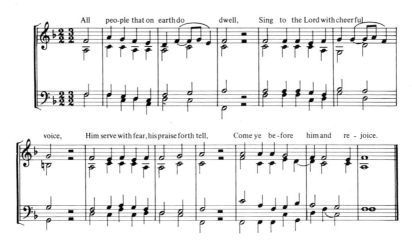

Despite having insisted on 'understanding' in church, the Queen saw clearly that religious fanatics could be attracted to a faith which was proclaimed in Geneva as 'a church of the people' and that sooner or later the conflict of loyalties between such a church and herself could be as acute for Puritans as it was for Roman Catholics.

So she continued to follow a middle course, outwardly favourable to the established church, saying:

"If I were not certain that mine were the true way to God's will, God forbid that I should live to prescribe it to you."

Some Puritans faced trial in the Tower; Roman Catholics could be tolerated provided that their loyalty could be seen; and the Queen remained in people's minds as God's 'Anointed Queen'. The special prayer offered by the Knights of the Garter each year reminded the inner circle of the Court of their allegiance.

This is the second part down in Day's setting of the *Old Hundredth* seen above, as it was printed in 1563. The familiar tune is in the third line down—the tenor—at a pitch most men in the congregation could sing. Women sang it as best they could at their own pitch. Choirs, if any, provided the parts but no doubt some families tried to join in with the 'descant' or 'bass' or sang all four parts at home.

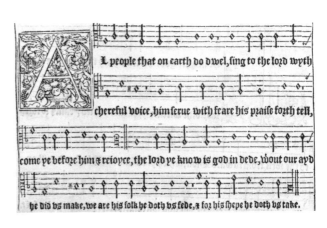

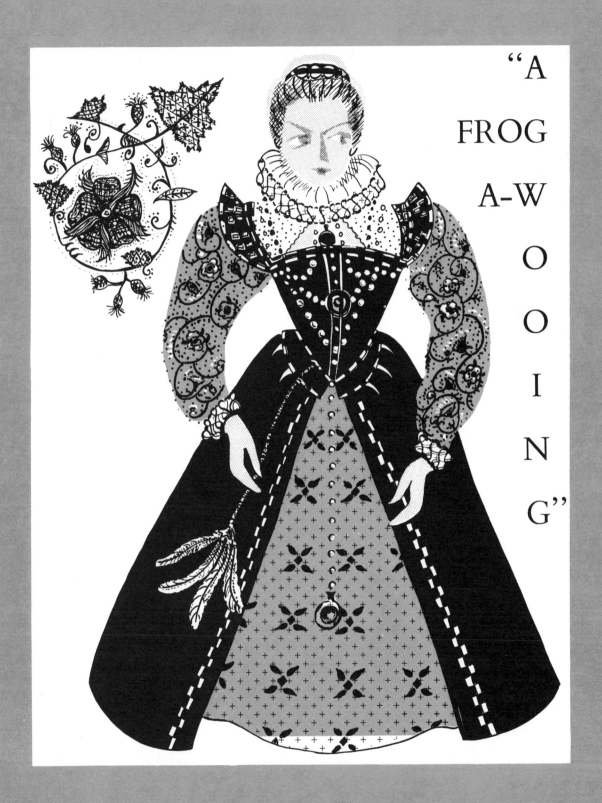

"A FROG A-WOOING"

To the Church and people, Elizabeth was 'The Virgin Queen'; to the inner circle of her courtiers, she was 'The Sun Queen'. Certainly she must have appeared to shine in her gorgeous bejewelled dresses and she expected all those who attended court—men and women—to wear beautiful clothes with ear-rings, jewels, chains of gold and ruffs of fine lace. Above all, they had to keep up with the fashions of Italy and France.

The chief courtiers in 1580 were the 60-year-old Lord Burghley (top), who had served Elizabeth since she was first granted her own estate as Princess in 1550; Sir Francis Walsingham (left), formerly Ambassador in Paris and now the Principal Secretary of State; and Sir Christopher Hatton (right), who had become one of the Queen's favourites in the 1570s, starting the usual gossip about her marital intentions.

LORD Robert Dudley, the 'Gipsy', had finally been created Earl of Leicester by the Queen—and given vast estates from crown lands—in 1564 and was still one of her favourites. She had disappointed the gossips in 1562 by not elevating him to the earldom. At that time he was still widely believed to have arranged the murder of his first wife; by 1564 he was even a possible husband for Mary, Queen of Scots, in Elizabeth's political judgment. Although nothing came of this notion, there was never any doubt about his closeness to the English throne—or at least to its occupant.

Leicester, Burghley, Walsingham and Hatton were the principal advisers, the centre of the court in 1580. Together with other councillors, the permanent civil servants and household officers they formed an all-male society accompanying the Queen wherever she held court. She had in her personal retinue twelve ladies of the nobility and six maids of honour (who hoped for noble husbands as a result of their service at Court). All these were obliged to be at Court unless the Queen herself gave them leave of absence.

Noblemen from all over England, Wales and Scotland were encouraged to attend as often as possible, bringing plenty of gifts and money to spend; sons of the nobility were sent as pages and 'apprenticed' to the court. Wives and daughters came only by invitation on grand occasions.

The Main Gateway to Hampton Court Palace. Reproduced by gracious permission of Her Majesty the Queen.

Sunday was the favourite day for being seen at Court. In the region of London, this might have meant travelling to any of fourteen different places, among them Whitehall, St. James's, Windsor, Hampton Court, Somerset House in the Strand and the Queen's favourite, Greenwich (where she was born). These places are still on the itinerary of many modern visitors to London but only Windsor and Hampton Court can still show the same face. They were all on or near the river Thames, for travelling by water was by far the easiest way to transport the vast domestic resources—food, fuel and furniture as well as staff—which were always taken from place to place.

The Presence Chamber, Hampton Court Palace. Reproduced by gracious permission of Her Majesty the Queen.

Before Chapel, even on an ordinary Sunday, the procession from the presence chamber was very impressive, beginning with nobles all in order of precedence, then the Lord Keeper of the Seal bearing it in a red silk purse, followed by the Sword of State, the Sceptre and finally Her Majesty with her ladies in waiting and maids of honour. In many of her palaces, the procession would pass between lines of visitors to the court and in the larger ones also through crowds of sightseers, all of whom had to kneel—on both knees—as she passed.

Once in the Chapel, Her Majesty could only be glimpsed in her gallery, usually in the west end. The sermon might well have been lively if the Queen disagreed, for she often brought a preacher in full flight to earth by a rasping "To your text, Mr. Preacher". Elizabeth still maintained the choir of the Chapel Royal as a royal showpiece, and their elaborate part-singing was famous.

Outside Court services, however, a visitor was seldom likely to hear the 'Golden Age' of polyphony composed by members of the Elizabethan Chapel Royal. The *only* printed music of this kind available was a set of *Cantiones Sacrae* by Tallis and Byrd which the two composers published when they were given the first monopoly by the Queen to print 'pricksong' in 1575. These were a commercial failure and, being Catholic motets, they were unlikely to be otherwise in English cathedrals.

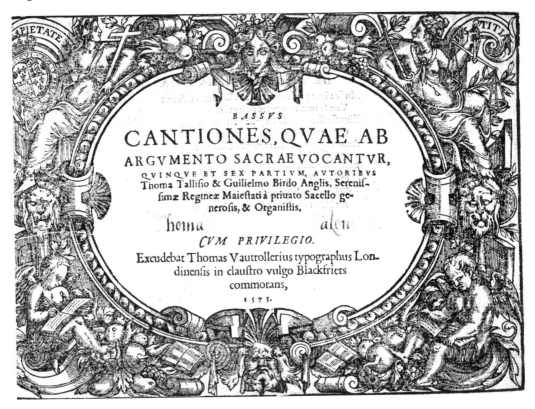

After Chapel, straight to dinner at midday. This had been laid out with great ceremony (like that described on pages 25 and 26), accompanied by trumpets and drums, in the presence chamber for the Royal Table and at various high officials' tables in hall besides. The Royal apartments, for security reasons, were always on the first floor of palaces and a lady taster examined each dish before anything was sent through to the Queen, who on most Sundays dined alone or with one or two of her ladies in the Privy Chamber. Although the Queen ate little and drank less, the choice of fare at a simple Court Dinner was ample if not exotic, typically including:

Soup

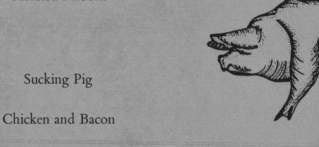

Roast Lamb

Peahen

Roasted Rabbits

Sucking Pig

Chicken and Bacon

Roast Veal

Salt, spiced Beef

Roast Beef

and   Garlic

Baked Venison Tart

Savoury 'Yorkshire Pudding'

The total number attending or serving the Court has been calculated from contemporary lists of establishment at about 1500. According to Royal Household accounts, in one year they ate 60,000 pounds of butter, over 33,000 chickens, over 20,000 sheep and lambs, over 4,000 oxen, cows and calves, 310 pigs and 560 flitches of bacon.

Part of the Kitchens, Hampton Court Palace. Reproduced by gracious permission of Her Majesty the Queen.

For many, such a dinner must have preceded a sleepy afternoon but not necessarily for the Queen, who received ambassadors, suitors and petitioners on many a Sunday. Others might walk in the grounds or the maze, arguing, intriguing, plotting . . . and above all else, gossiping.

The Queen was 46 and unmarried. She had twice been seriously ill and her careless attitude to security—in loving to be in crowds and in accepting gifts from strangers—meant that, to her courtiers, there was always a nagging question of "what if Her Majesty dies?" Lightheartedly, courtiers had been taking bets on different suitors for twenty years, from foreign kings and archdukes in the early days (Spain, Sweden, France and Austria) to the ever-present favourite at home, the Earl of Leicester. But by 1580 it really looked as if the Queen would remain unmarried.

Leicester, to the Queen's displeasure, had married secretly two years before and the only name to bet on was Francis, Duke of Alençon. He had been to England (supposedly incognito, though betting had been two to one against his coming) in 1579 and Elizabeth, according to gossip, was truly in love . . . with a 28-year old Frenchman. Puritan anger in the Church stirred up the feelings of ordinary people against this French Catholic, playing on the fears of a return to the past; the Privy Council was divided. Whatever her true feelings, the Queen knew she could not marry her 'Frog Prince'. Politically, however, she had to play the game of courtship, needing the friendship of France against the growing menace of Spain.

So the gossip continued, followed in the evening by dancing. Often the Queen herself would lead the dance, no doubt with Hatton (first noticed for his elegant step and now a spritely 41). One erstwhile favourite who had made Hatton so jealous for one year with his 'dancing and valiantness' when he arrived at Court in 1572, was conspicuously absent in 1580: court gossip earlier in the year had proved true and the Earl of Oxford had indeed fathered a child of one of Elizabeth's maids of honour. The unfortunate girl was still in the Tower.

Dancing, as with eating, began with great ceremony. First were the 'grave measures' of the Pavan (still a procession for all those intending to dance), then Corantos and Galliards.

Although this dance was named 'The Frog Galliard' with reference to Alençon 'a-wooing', it is actually a Coranto. It was also a song about Alençon's going back to France, beginning "Now, O now I needs must part" with the rejected suitor's refrain:

"Sad despair doth drive me hence; this despair unkindness sends.
If that parting be offence, it is she that then offends".

With the Volta, the atmosphere probably grew more informal:

"Yet there is one, the most delightful kind
A lofty jumping and a leaping round
When arm in arm two dancers are entwined
And whirl themselves, with strict embracements bound.
And still their feet an anapaest do sound—
An anapaest is all their music's song,
Whose first two feet are short
And third is long."

The white fur of the ermine became a symbol of chastity through its association with the 'Virgin Queen'. This drawing shows the ermine on one of Elizabeth's dresses as it appears in a portrait at Hatfield House, attributed to William Segar.

By now, music for dancing was played either on pipe and tabor (see page 53) or by a 'broken consort' (see page 83). This dance, and the Coranto before it, are arranged for six instruments. The parts as numbered would originally have been played by:

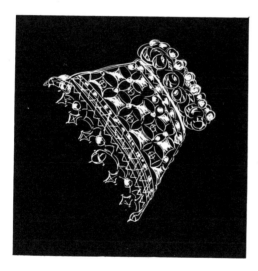

1. Violin

2. Tenor Flute

3. Bass Viol

4. Lute (line 3 also), with pandora and cittern playing the chords indicated between lines 3 and 4.

It can be re-created today by any combination of melody instruments playing lines 1, 2 and 3, with guitar (or even soft piano) adding the chords. For the full dance, the sections are repeated AABBAABB, not too quickly, emphasising the ending of each section as shown, to give what the poet heard as "short-short, long"—the opposite of the pavan (see page 16).

The Volta was the only dance in which a couple faced each other in each other's arms, potentially as immoral as the waltz became 250 years later. Elizabeth greatly enjoyed it. The drawing on the next page—probably not of the Queen since its origin is French—shows how the jumping turn ('volta' in Italian) needed support from the gentleman.

51

Now they were ready for the 'Country Dances', which used old tunes and which in general allowed every man to dance with every woman as well as his own partner. The evening might well end with a kissing game—kissing was very popular with the Elizabethans—to the tune of "The Cushion Dance".

linked for progression by:

Played AA BB AA

to AA etc.

The directions given for dancing this Cushion Dance in Playford's *Dancing Master* (1651 onwards) may or may not have dated back to the days of Elizabeth, but this tune certainly did. A country dance adopted by the Court, the lady chose each partner by setting the cushion before him. In some houses even servants joined in this dance, causing a character in a play called *A Woman killed with Kindness* (1602) to complain of his "hall floor pecked and dinted like a millstone with their high shoes".

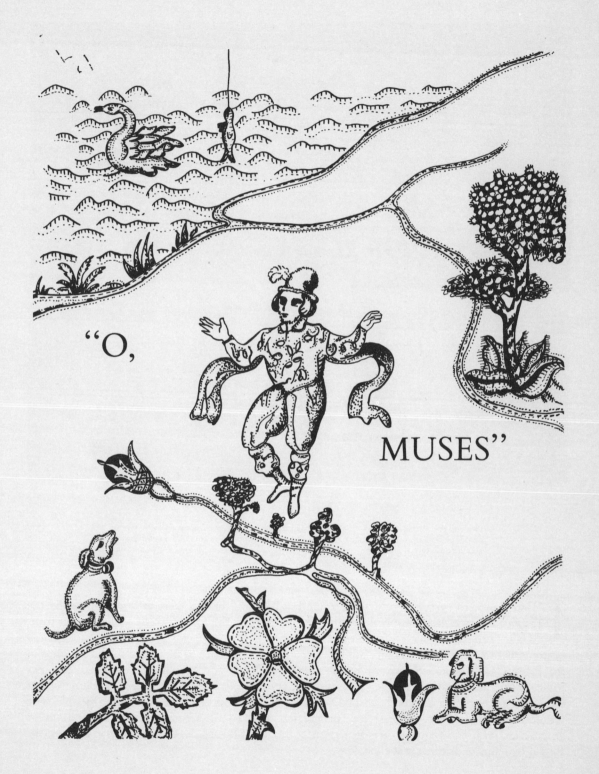

"O,

MUSES"

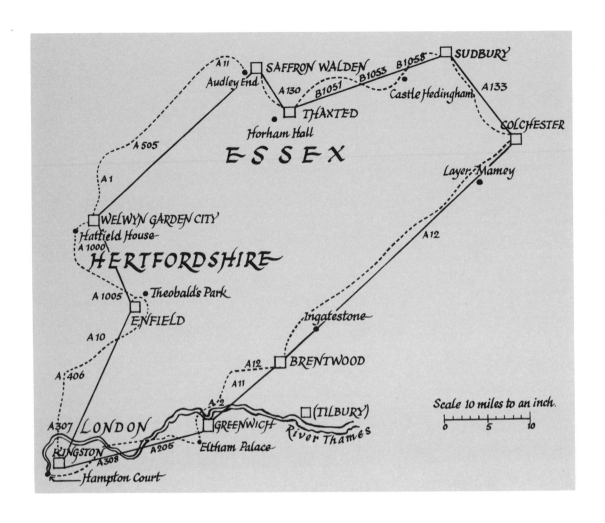

One of the Progress routes through Hertfordshire and Essex, showing places where estates or buildings of the time may still be seen. Modern road numbers show the easiest round route today.

FROM 1560 to 1580, except in 1562 when England and France were at war and during the first of the two great outbreaks of the plague in 1563, the Queen went on a summer tour. These 'progresses' were often described in letters from eye-witnesses (sometimes greatly exaggerated to impress the reader) but the facts behind them are to be found in the Minutes of the Privy Council, since the Council was always with her and meetings were held in every palace, castle and house. With her, too, were many of the more distinguished noblemen from the London court, for Elizabeth wished to bring as rich a spectacle as possible to people who would never see London. At least 500 'progressed' in her train across the countryside in up to 30 coaches, with 300 baggage carts and about a thousand horses. As in her London palaces, the Royal bed and bedclothes travelled, too.

The splendid procession inevitably moved slowly and normally set out in the morning to cover about ten miles, reaching the next house or palace in time for midday dinner. This allowed Her Majesty to stay two nights in each place, with one full day for holiday entertainment. In her own palaces such as Hatfield or very large estates such as Audley End, she stayed a day or two longer. With few exceptions, the houses she stayed at belonged to the 'new gentry'. They were the sons and descendants of nobles and knights created by her father, Henry VIII, rewarded with confiscated monastic lands, treasures and compulsorily acquired Catholic properties. Not many of them remained rich after receiving the Queen on progress, but there was a saving on the Royal Accounts.

Photo. David L. Lipson, Dunmow.

The unfortunate grandson of Henry VIII's treasurer, Sir John Cutte, was honoured by *two* visitations at Horham Hall. The first of these lasted nine days because of a political crisis, when Burghley felt it wiser for Her Majesty to stay where she was. After the second visit in 1578, the Cutte family went bankrupt.

Although fairly small houses such as Horham could accommodate the Queen with her Council and immediate retinue, there was little hope of housing all 500 in spite of the extra building the owners put up. When there was no large town nearby to provide lodgings, many courtiers would have to sleep in outhouses or even under canvas like an army in the grounds. It is small wonder that some elderly knights complained of the evils of 'progress'.

The anxious host, with the help of his more wealthy neighbours, also had to provide the entertainment. For music, a few families employed their own musicians in the household but most had to hire them. Horham was at least within reasonable distance of Cambridge and the Waits there had a good consort, but elsewhere the local musicians were not up to the refined style to which the Court was accustomed and the family themselves might better show off their musical sons and daughters on the lute or virginals.

This variation on the tune of the 'Frog Galliard' (see pages 48 and 49) was written towards the end of Elizabeth's reign or even after by John Wilbye, a musician employed by a family in Norfolk from c. 1595. A rich Cambridge undergraduate, Clement Matchett, copied it into his private book of virginal music in 1612. Variations like this formed the family albums on which young ladies—and some gentlemen—learnt to play.

This falconer would have kept his falcons in large holes in walls with mesh doors, such as those by the lake side at Horham Hall. The keen-eyed birds were trained to hunt all game birds.

Perhaps the cheapest and most popular entertainment for a host to organise was falconry (of which Elizabeth was very fond) or, for the sport of young courtiers, a hunt—although this could be costly if, like Cutte, the host had built a tower on the house for the Queen to watch from, only to find her riding to the chase herself.

Hunting parties were usually arranged in honour of the ladies, the lady of highest rank being expected to cut the dead stag first, before the rest was left to the huntsman.

Hey ho [whistle_____]

A mark,___ a mark!

Hey, soy dogs,soy dogs!

Whirr, hey dogs,hey dogs!

Many writers have thought that this drawing shows the Queen herself 'taking the first cut'. The saying still with us today bears witness to the Queen's financial acumen (see page 70), in its modern usage.

Ret Chance, hey ret for tune. hut,hut,hut.

Ware hawk,warehawk,warehawk.

60

A magnificent hunt formed part of one of the most memorable entertainments of Elizabeth's reign, organised by Leicester at the height of his popularity in 1575. This progress to Kenilworth Castle—one of the Queen's presents to 'Sweet Robin'—drew folk from all over the Midlands.

Tink – a-tink, tink – a-tink, tink – a-tink, tink.

tink – a-tink, tink – a-tink, tink – a-tink, tink.

Have you a-ny work for a tin – ker?

Gipsies, beggars, shepherds, tinkers, cobblers, sellers of all kinds of trinkets, yeoman farmers with their families, and merchants from Stratford and Warwick all came to see the Queen and to marvel at the splendour of the Court.

Sweet ju-ni-per, ju-ni-per!

Gar – lic, good Gar – lic!

Broom,   broom, broom.   will you buy an – y   broom?

Salt, ⌐ salt, salt,   salt   Fine white salt, fine!

Buy   an-y ink,will you buy an-y ink,   buy an-y ve-ry fine wri-ting ink,will you buy an-y ink and pens?

Ve-ry fine Ve-nice glass-es!

Ha' ye an-y corns on your feet or   toes?

There were pastoral plays about Phoebus and Pan with flute accompaniment and old-style minstrels declaiming to the harp.

"O Muses, now come help me to rejoice since Jove has changed my grief to sudden joy" sang Diana in the greenwood.

The Muses came daily, even on the lake, where one evening during a grand water show mythical figures sang on the back of a 24-foot dolphin, accompanied by a consort of six musicians in its belly. The covered-in barge may have amplified the sound but the players must have been very hot and sticky. A Lady of the Lake completed the allusion to King Arthur.

1. Kites

2. Popgun

3. Hobby-horse

4. Alphabet board

5. Hoop

6. Embroidery

7. Skittles

8. Hand-ball

9. Whip

10. Sticks

Some games, pastimes and 'homework' (no. 4) for Elizabethan children.

On the Sunday afternoon there was a village wedding in the local church, to which musicians and Morris dancers went 'in ancient style'. Just as villagers had never seen court splendour, many courtiers had probably never witnessed a village wedding.

Although this is a university song, this is the kind of round (or catch, each voice chasing the other) which greeted Elizabeth on progress. The third entry is the motto of the Order of the Garter (see page 31): "The shame be his who thinks ill of it". "Long live England" and "Long live Queen Elizabeth" were known in these Latin forms even by country people (such as those drawn on the previous two pages).

Hunting, bear-baiting and dancing filled the days; music, drama and fireworks the evenings. Occasionally the English weather brought an excuse to rest but it says much for Elizabeth's stamina that she rode to the hunt the day before she left and could still patiently suffer yet another singer in the greenwood, introduced this time as 'Deep Desire' with the ubiquitous hidden orchestra, bidding farewell:

"Come, Muses and help us to lament."

Early next morning she started for Chartley over 50 miles to the North, which was to be the furthest north she would ever travel in her life. With Bristol the westerly limit, Norwich to the east and Southampton southernmost, the Queen had by 1580 travelled through roughly a third of England.

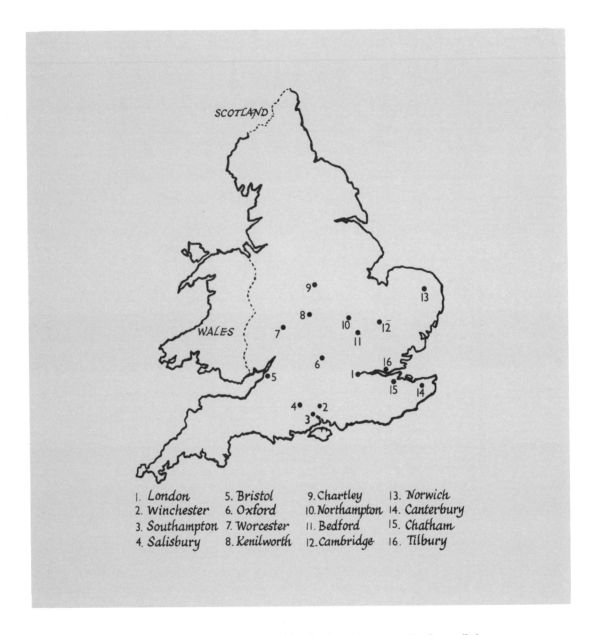

1. London	5. Bristol	9. Chartley	13. Norwich
2. Winchester	6. Oxford	10. Northampton	14. Canterbury
3. Southampton	7. Worcester	11. Bedford	15. Chatham
4. Salisbury	8. Kenilworth	12. Cambridge	16. Tilbury

This map shows the boundaries covered by the Queen's progresses. In almost all the towns shown there are still memorials of the Queen's visit to be seen or read in the public libraries.

"I DO;
YET
DARE
NOT
SAY"

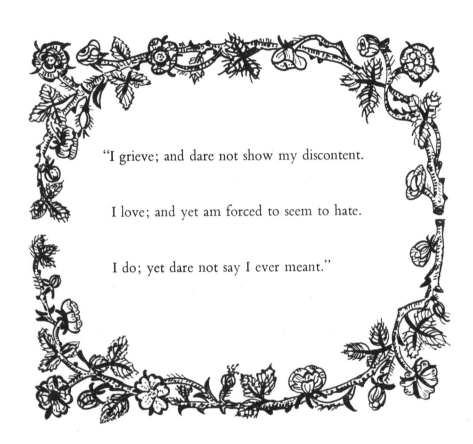

"I grieve; and dare not show my discontent.

I love; and yet am forced to seem to hate.

I do; yet dare not say I ever meant."

QUEEN Elizabeth knew the poetry of Petrarch. When she penned these lines in imitation of the early sonnets, they were taken to refer to the end of the Alençon affair and to form part of the huge collection of love letters which passed between them. But they were also remarkably apt to her heartache over one whose life was to be ended by the executioner.

Mary Stuart, former Queen of Scotland. The love and hate seemed equally divided in each cousin.

In 1585, ten years after Elizabeth Tudor visited Chartley, her cousin Mary Stuart, former Queen of Scotland, was taken there. The passionate Catholic had been in 'protective custody' for 17 years, mostly at Tutbury (only twelve miles from Chartley). Her son was the Scottish king and she still considered herself the rightful Queen of England. She was also nine years younger than Elizabeth.

Rebellion was in the air. Walsingham, in charge of spies and counter-spies alike, discovered the secrets of what Catholics called 'the Enterprise'. By October, the Queen agreed to Mary's trial for having supported a plan to assassinate her. The country was alive with ballads about it.

After much hesitation, partly from personal emotion and partly from political uncertainty, Elizabeth eventually signed the death warrant on February the 1st, 1587. One week later, with great courage, the former heir to the thrones of France and Scotland and claimant to that of England, died on the block.

Even traitors went to their deaths with music. The folk-tune "Joan's Placket" is the basis of this piper's lament which only popular legend associates with the death of Mary Stuart. But stranger legends than this have proved musically true and Highland laments defy historical explanation.

Three of Elizabeth's most successful admirals. Only Lord Howard of Effingham, later Earl of Nottingham (top), was born into the nobility. The other two were West Country 'gentlemen'—born buccaneers—who were turned into courtiers by service in the Queen's name: Sir Francis Drake (left) and Sir Walter Raleigh (right).

The prospect of a Catholic rebellion was over but war with Spain was inevitable. Courtiers going to war were heroes for their Queen and Country, not for any particular religion, and the adventure would bring either death . . . or glory . . . and profit.

When Drake returned to England in the late Spring of 1587, having "singed the King of Spain's beard" by destroying part of the Spanish Fleet in harbour, he also arrived with £140,000 in treasure captured from a Portuguese galleon on the way home. The royal dividend was

Musicians even went to sea and Drake had a group of viol players in his crew. This pavan, known as the Spanish dance, probably came back with groups of this kind. John Bull, another musician who served Elizabeth abroad, called it 'The Spanish Pavan'. Its origins must lie with the harmonic pattern of earlier Spanish lute music.

£40,000 or, in terms of today's money, £2 million. The dividing line between acts of war and piracy had long been thin and Drake owed his knighthood as much to the money he had 'earned' for Her Majesty as to his courage and seamanship.

In 1588 the Spanish Fleet arrived in the Channel to pave the way for invasion by troops from Holland.

Queen Elizabeth rides to address her troops at Tilbury. The commander of the invasion defences was the Earl of Leicester, by then a sick man performing the last of his thirty years' service. Within weeks, 'Sweet Robin' was dead.

With the crushing defeat of the Armada, the soldiers were not needed. They could, however, always tell their children how the Queen came to inspect them and inspire them with such memorable words as:

"I am come amongst you . . . not for my recreation . . . but being resolved . . . to live or die amongst you all"

and

"I have the body of a weak and feeble woman, but I have the heart and stomach of a King."

For the rest of her reign, Elizabeth's courtiers were expected to show their courage by volunteering to serve her either on land (in Ireland, Normandy, the Netherlands) or at sea. Musicians duly recorded the mood of the time in popular song:

1. Stand to it, no-ble pike — men and look you round a — bout; and
2. shoot you right, you bow — men and we will keep them

out; you mus-ket and ca - li - ver men, do you prove true to me and

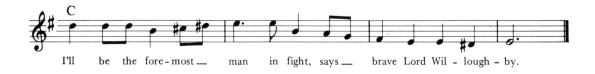

I'll be the fore - most — man in fight, says — brave Lord Wil - lough - by.

'Good Peregrine' as the Queen called Lord Willoughby, succeeded Leicester in command of the army in the Netherlands and became the symbol of bravery to troops and people alike, as this very popular ballad showed.

and in these sophisticated 'variations':

This variation for virginals is another example of the popularity of 'keyboard arrange-ments' of well-known tunes to be played by ladies and gentlemen for themselves or to friends. The letters ABC trace the variations against the tune opposite.

Life at Court in war-time was becoming sour for the Queen. Leicester, Walsingham and Hatton were all dead and only Burghley, in his seventies, remained of her old Council. Even fantastic celebrations at Elvetham in 1591 on the lines of the Kenilworth progress fell a little flat; aquatic celebration with Titon and odes to Gloriana were too reminiscent of Leicester and by now sonnets to the Queen's beauty were harder to credit. The masks and pageants had become dull and even vulgar to her.

Edmund Spenser, formerly in the Earl of Leicester's household, served the Queen in Ireland, and became a firm friend of the Earl of Essex.

Spenser's *Faerie Queene*, the finest poem in English since Chaucer's *Canterbury Tales*, appears to have been unknown to most of the court though it was published about 1589 and the Queen personally—having had parts read to her by the poet—showed little enthusiasm. It was left to Spenser to get his own back:

> "Full little knowest thou that hast not tried
> What Hell it is in suing long to bide;
> To lose good days that might be better spent,
> To waste long nights in pensive discontent;
> To speed today, to be put back tomorrow,
> To feed on hope, to pine with fear and sorrow;
> To have thy Prince's grace yet want her Peer's,
> To have thy asking, yet wait many years;
> To fret thy soul with crosses and with cares,
> To eat thy heart through comfortless despairs;
> To fawn, to crouch, to wait, to ride, to run,
> To spend, to give, to want, to be undone".

The disenchanted Raleigh, poet, made it shorter:

> "Say to the Court, it glows;
> and shines like rotten wood."

Blood sports—dogs against bulls or bears particularly—were the delight of most young courtiers, who thought little of their own time and even less about their future:

Of all jol-ly pas-times good fellows do use, Bull baiting is best I like it to choose.Of choose

hold thy own my dog   And then they cry

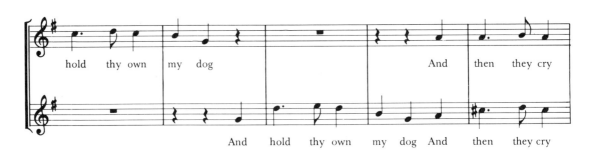

'Bow - wow' and   then   they   cry   'Bow - wow'.

Repeat line 1 to finish

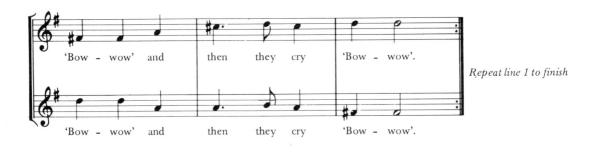

'Bow - wow' and   then   they   cry   'Bow - wow'.

Bear baiting and bull baiting alternated with plays in the South Bank 'entertainments'. A bear, its teeth broken, was tied to a stake and four or five mastiffs were let loose on it. Gentlemen would bet on the dogs against the bears—where the odds were low on the bear—or on the bulls where the odds were higher. The terms 'bulls' and 'bears' for those who speculate on the Stock Exchange probably have their origins in this gambling.

Robert Devereux, second Earl of Essex.

Only the Earl of Essex, firmly established at the Queen's side by 1591, believed that the next decade would be his. The stepson of the Earl of Leicester, he was in his early twenties and only too ready to obey the call to arms with natural bloodthirstiness, high ambition and no illusions, saying:

"I will adventure to be rich;
if not, I will not live to see
the end of my poverty."

"WHAT THOU WILT HEAR?"

ONE Courtier was determined that the Court should have worthwhile music and drama. Lord Oxford, having survived his period of disgrace in the 1580s, had succeeded by various subterfuges in keeping a school of music and drama going for Her Majesty's Children in Blackfriars. Since the landlord of the former monastery of the Black Friars was a stern Puritan who hated the theatre, the choirboys from Windsor and St. Paul's housed and educated there officially learned only to sing in addition to the normal school subjects.

Edward de Vere, Earl of Oxford (see page 48).

By 1585, however, the children were appearing at Court Revels as 'The Earl of Oxford's Children' acting in Italian plays which the Earl brought back from his travels and plays which he probably wrote for them but ascribed to his secretary, John Lyly. When the City landlord found out that they were training as actors, the 'Blackfriars Children' were evicted. But by then the new buildings opened for the Master of the Revels in the north of the City were able to accommodate them . . . and the Master then appointed was the Earl of Oxford himself.

The terrible plague which began in 1592 raged throughout London in 1593 and over 10,000 deaths were recorded in the year. When public life began slowly to revive in 1594, it was as if war itself had devastated the City. Public buildings (including inns) which had been closed were tumbling down, the few theatres among them; and in all 'companies'—whether of merchants, craftsmen or actors—the survivors were, as one of them wrote, "like so many starved snakes".

The Corporation of London had never licensed a public theatre and sought to chase out actors who had been used to playing in inn yards.

With his two friends, Howard (the Lord High Admiral, in whose ships he had served in 1588) and Hunsdon (the Lord Chamberlain), Lord Oxford now managed to get the Court of Common Council (that is, The Corporation) to agree to license two companies of actors. Each would be guaranteed by the two Privy Councillors as law-abiding and the plays would be subject to censorship by the Lord Chamberlain. For the first time in England, professional actors were recognised by law. And they were no longer vagabonds, since each company was allotted an official theatre.

'The Lord Chamberlain's Men' were given the Theatre under Richard Burbage (left), whose father had borrowed £30,000 in our money to put up the building in 1576. Edward Alleyn (right) was actor-manager of 'The Lord Admiral's Men' in the Rose on Bankside. In 1599 Burbage moved his theatre—using much of the old timber—to Bankside, as the Globe; in the following year Alleyn opened the Fortune in Barbican (see pages 105 and 108).

The marvellous success of this enterprise brought Elizabeth's court back to life with a blood-rush of new plays, most of which were acted before the Court as nowhere else in Europe. The Queen, with Essex at her side, watched what was perhaps Lord Oxford's finest hour, the performance of a new play just before his daughter's wedding in 1594: *A Midsummer Night's Dream*. It is pleasing to think that the companies of his two friends played the courtiers and rustics (each having been able to rehearse separately) whilst his own 'Children' (of Her Majesty's Chapel and St. Paul's) sang, played recorders and acted the fairies in this tailor-made play. No mention was made of the 'tailor' but only two men were paid for the performance: Mr. Richard Burbage and Mr. William Shakespeare.

The Children of the Chapel were the successors of those who first performed 'Choirboy Plays' in the 1550s. In *Damon and Pythias* (one of the earliest plays), the hero ends: "Loth am I to depart. O Music, sound my doleful plaints when I am gone away". This was to be followed by "a mourning song" which has not survived. These final, dying songs became known as 'Loth-to-departs' and were duly recorded in virginal music such as that above. A later round echoes the title page reproduced here: "Sing with thy mouth, sing with thy heart, like *faithful friends*, sing Loth to Depart". Shakespeare parodies the never-ending song when Pyramus takes so long to die in *A Midsummer Night's Dream* (see also page 104).

Musical directions in Elizabethan plays from the earliest days of *Gorboduc* tell us when music was a normal part of ceremonial life. Sometimes instruments are specified but since players either learnt by rote (as the trumpeters and drummers certainly did) or played from long-lost manuscripts (as the theatre orchestra probably did) we can only guess at the actual music. Thomas Morley's *Consort Lessons*, published in 1599, gives us a rare glimpse of what the best theatre orchestra could do.

These 'lessons' were in fact arrangements of tunes played by the City Waits and include a setting of "O, Mistress Mine" (a song used later by Shakespeare in *Twelfth Night*). The Waits played in the 'official' theatres but their music in this collection may have been intended as 'lessons' for amateurs to copy them. A famous picture of a musical gentleman's life story painted for his widow and dating from 1597, however, shows us that the particular combination was that of a professional band.

The musicians, from left to right round the table, play violin, tenor flute, lute, cittern (a small guitar for chord work like a ukulele), bass viol and—his back to the painter—pandora (bass guitar), These are Morley's instruments in the *Consort Lessons* and make up a 'broken' consort (see page 51) since they came from different families: blown, bowed and plucked.

The same picture plainly shows an amateur group playing viols to accompany a boy singer.

The player on the right looks like the head of the household, Sir Henry Umpton. The
choirboy singing with his back to us may well have been hired for the evening.

It was quite usual for a gentleman to include playing the viol among his accomplishments, but
if he had guests who did not play (or if there were not enough instruments to go round) they
could sing instrumental parts to sol-fa syllables—or they could all sing madrigals. If they wished,
they could also play madrigals on the viols.

This refrain from Morley's *First Book of Balletts* (1595) shows the sort of all-purpose writing to nonsense syllables which was a feature of early madrigals. 'Light' music greatly out-numbers 'grave' in the madrigal collections published before 1600.

"COME AWAY, COME AWAY, DEATH"

BY the end of the century, Robert, Earl of Essex had indeed become a popular hero but it was at the expense of his position at Court. He obviously shared Raleigh's disenchantment, as this song shows:

It was   a   Time   when sil – ly bees could speak,
Then thus   I   buzz'd   when Thyme no sap would give,
'My liege gods grant   thy Time may nev – er   end,

And   in that Time   I   was   a   sil – ly bee,
Why should this bless – – ed Thyme to   me   be dry
And yet vouch-safe   to   hear my plaint of Thyme,

Who   fed   on Thyme un – til my heart 'gan break,   Yet
Sith by this Thyme the la – zy drone doth live,   The
Which fruit – less flies have found to have   a   friend, And

never found the Time would fav-our me.
wasp, the worm, the gnat, the but-ter-fly.
I cast down when at-om-ies* do climb',

Of all the swarm I on-ly did not thrive,
Ma-ted with grief, I kneel-ed on my knees,
The King re-plied but thus, 'Peace peev-ish bee,

mf

Yet brought I wax and hon-ey to the hive.
And thus com-plain'd un-to the King of bees.
Thou'rtbound to serve the Time, the Thyme not thee.'

*atomies = walking skeletons in Shakespeare's language.

Like Raleigh, the frustrated Essex turned to poetry to express his thoughts about the court. This is the setting of his words by John Dowland.

The Earl of Essex had adventured to be rich, but he was nearly bankrupt. Deliberately he set out 'not to see the end' of his poverty. Disdaining all secrecy, he planned a rebellion of 'the people' of London against the Queen's 'enemies'. The City of London refused him arms and his cause was lost. On Ash Wednesday 1601, Essex was executed. He was 33.

Sweet England's prize is gone! Well-a day, well-a day

Which makes her sigh and groan E-ver more still.

He did her fare ad-vance, in Ire-land, France and Spain

And by a sad mis-chance is from us ta'en,

This dirge was sung all over London and, no doubt, in many an army camp. Although the City Fathers had remained loyal, there were many young people—courtiers and commoners—to whom the dashing Earl of Essex was a symbol of the future, as they felt the unease of being governed by an older generation. The Queen's signature reproduced on page 22 is taken from the Earl's death warrant. She seemed strangely unmoved at his death.

Most courtiers were soon prepared to forget the 'sad mischance' of Essex's end. Once again gossip could concentrate unhindered on the maids of honour and marriage. By the Autumn, another seduced maid of honour had been punished by banishment and the Russian ambassador was asking the Queen to find a bride for his Emperor's son.

Parlament House   the Hall

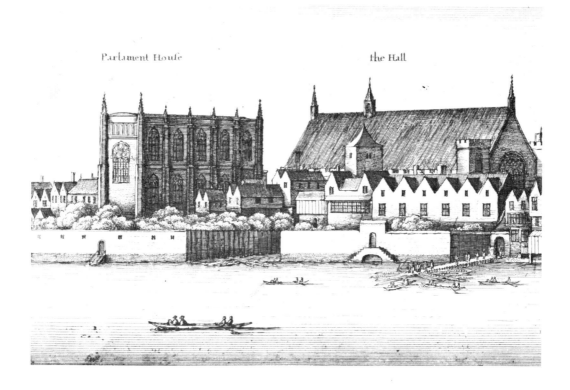

Another view of the Palace Hall at Westminster and the House in which Elizabeth addressed Parliament in 1601. See page 18.

At the end of the year, Elizabeth persuaded Parliament to raise heavy taxes to support her policies, partly by agreeing to look at the evils of monopolies by which certain people had the right to sell essential commodities such as coal, soap, salt and leather at whatever price they chose.

Thomas Morley, after intrigue worthy of any courtier, had acquired the music printing monopoly when Byrd's patent expired. Politic as ever, he asked twenty-three composers—mostly organists of the cathedrals and colleges which the Queen had visited on progresses, together with friends of his and of his printer living in the City—to write a madrigal each in homage to the Queen. The words in all cases were to end with 'Long live fair Oriana'.

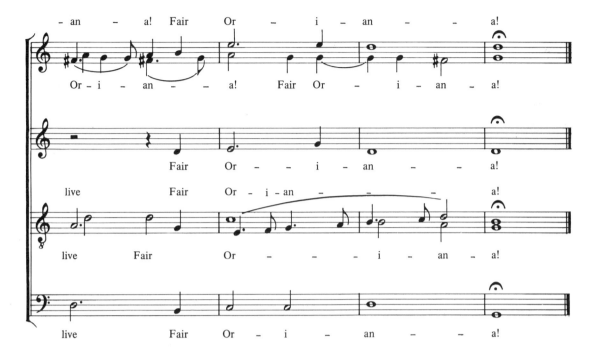

With exquisite tact, Morley dedicated his collection called *The Triumphs of Oriana* to Lord Admiral Howard . . . who was in charge of the enquiry into monopolies. This refrain comes at the end of "Fair Orian in the morn" contributed by John Milton, father of the poet, who was then an apprentice in the City.

The Court's appetite for dance music was insatiable and Morley's idea of a madrigal collection was old-fashioned. Though a few young composers contributed to it, most of them were too busy with chamber music, keyboard music and solo songs with lute or strings and most of their music was based upon the dance.

Much of the music published in 1603 reflects both the gaiety of the dance and the sadness of old age. No song captures this feeling better than one in Dowland's last book of lute songs, which was also to be the last book Morley published before he died.

Weep you no more, sad foun - tains What
Sleep is a re - con - cil - ing, A

need you flow so fast? Look how the snow - y
rest that Peace be - gets: Doth not the sun rise

moun - tains Heav'n's sun doth gen - tly waste.
smil - ing When fair at - e'en he sets.

But my sun's _____ heav'n — ly eyes
Rest you then, _____ rest, _____ sad eyes,

View not your weep – ing,
Melt not in weep – ing,

That now lies sleep – ing, that now lies sleep – ing, Soft — ly
While she lies sleep – ing, While she lies sleep – ing, Soft — ly,

soft — ly, now soft — ly lies _____ sleep – ing.
soft — ly, now soft — ly lies _____ sleep – ing.

95

Queen Elizabeth held her last illustrious audience on a typical Sunday at Court in her palace at Richmond. Dressed in silver and white taffeta trimmed with gold, wearing her Imperial crown and 'a vast quantity' of jewels, she received the first ambassador to be sent to her from Venice; and in the evening, to the Italian gentleman's surprise as it was Sunday, there was dancing.

Within a few weeks—on March the 24th, 1603—the Queen was dead. She enjoyed dancing almost till the end and even went hunting ten miles on horseback just before her 69th birthday. The theatre was alive and music was a constant companion in all walks of life. In death, it comforted and strengthened the mourners.

John Bull was the only Elizabethan composer known to have had his portrait painted whilst he was alive. A second portrait, painted in 1600 and formerly in the collection of Thurston Dart, is now in the National Portrait Gallery.

When the Queen died, Bull was listed at the head of the Gentlemen of the Chapel Royal and he paid his tribute . . . with a solemn Pavan. "Queen Elizabeth's Pavan", of which this is a part, makes a fitting musical end to the life of a Queen who, perhaps above all, loved dancing.

The drawings on this
page are by someone
present at the Queen's
Funeral. At the head,
the Queen's Horse was
led by two Equerries.

The Bishop of London.

The Sergeant of the Vestry.

Children of the Chapel.

The Lancaster Herald.

The Banner of Wales.

Wars and politics, religious and secular, had never been far away from Her Majesty all her life. Through her own love for the dance, drama and music she left the English court at the centre of European culture and a country seemingly at peace with itself and with its neighbours.

Courtiers and people looked north as James Stuart, King of Scotland, began his 400-mile progress from Edinburgh to the City of London to become their rightful sovereign. The crowds came in their thousands . . . particularly in the Midland towns where they had never seen their monarch. But never again did an English monarch hold such personal authority over the people of England as did "Fair Oriana".

SOURCES FOR PERFORMING ELIZABETHAN MUSIC

THE amount of music printed in Elizabethan times was very small. John Day (see pages 37 & 38) and his son Richard held a royal licence to print music from 1559 until 1603; Elizabeth also granted a monopoly to assign music to printers—and to import music—to Tallis and Byrd (see page 44). Printers 'by assignment' from this monopoly included Vautrollier (see page 44) and later, in Morley's monopoly (see page 92), Barley, East and Short. Apart from these printers we have only the manuscript collections of patrons and gentlemen who compiled their own anthologies in the early seventeenth century, transcribed for the virginals. No music was *printed* for virginals until 1612.

These were imaginary portraits to do honour to the first two holders of the Royal patent to publish printed music, made several years after they died.

Any other knowledge of what music sounded like at the Court of Elizabeth I must be conjecture, based on description and deduction. All the known music is now available in *Musica Britannica* (published for the Royal Musical Association), *Early English Church Music* (published for the British Academy), and the company publications of Stainer and Bell: *The English Madrigalists*, *The English Lute-Songs*, *The Collected Works of William Byrd*, and *Early English Keyboard Music*.

The music reproduced in the book comes from the following:

73	"Rowland" or "Lord Willoughby's Welcome Home" by William Byrd. This is the opening, transposed for comparison with the ballad tune. The complete set of variations are edited by Alan Brown in *Musica Brittanica* Volume XXVII and by Thurston Dart in *Early Keyboard Music*, book 4.
76	The vocal parts only of an anonymous setting for voice and viols in The British Museum, Add. MSS. 17786–91. Philip Brett has a complete transcription in his edition of *Musica Britannica* Volume XXII.
82	The first strain of Giles Farnaby's "Loath to Depart" from *Early Keyboard Music*, book 11.
84, 85 & 86	Available in *English Madrigalists*, book 4 edited by Fellowes (rev. Dart) and in *Invitation to Madrigals*, book 6, edited by David Scott. In this three-stave version all parts sing 'la' to every note without a syllable in the refrains.
88 & 89	From Dowland's *Third Book of Songs*. The Fellowes edition with the original tablature has the song in *The English Lute Songs* book 10/11 and is included by David Scott in *Fifty Songs by John Dowland*, book 2. Dowland's own setting as a partsong accompanied by lute (four voices) is in *Musica Brittannica* Volume VI, edited by Thurston Dart and Nigel Fortune.
90	The ballad words are in the Roxburghe Collection. The tune is called "Essex's Last Goodnight" in Elizabeth Rogers' Virginal Book (collected as late as 1656, now in the British Museum Add. MSS. 10337) and was known as 'Well-a-day'.
92 & 93	*The Triumphs of Oriana* is published complete as *The English Madrigalists*, book 32.
94 & 95	From Dowland's *Third Book of Songs* (1603). See Sources, pages 88 & 89.
97	The complete Pavan is transcribed and edited by Thurston Dart in *Musica Britannica* Volume XIX.

SOURCES FOR STAGING ELIZABETHAN PLAYS

AUDIENCES, whether at Court entertainments or in the public playhouses, liked words—rhetoric and poetry—and fast action. The stage itself was a very flexible series of acting areas between which characters could move easily and without any pause for scene-changing. Scenery, in the modern sense, was used only on special occasions at Court, or in the Temple, where no permanent set was available; the public theatres relied on their large number of acting areas.

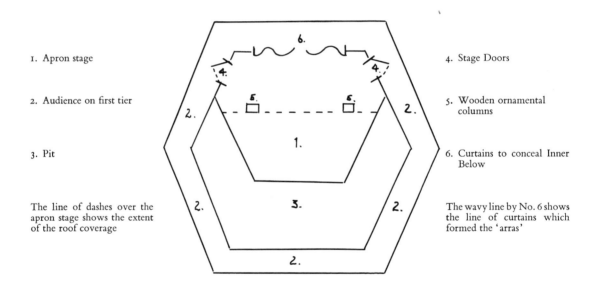

1. Apron stage

2. Audience on first tier

3. Pit

The line of dashes over the apron stage shows the extent of the roof coverage

4. Stage Doors

5. Wooden ornamental columns

6. Curtains to conceal Inner Below

The wavy line by No. 6 shows the line of curtains which formed the 'arras'

The only solid piece of painted scenery which seems to be unavoidable in Shakespeare's Elizabethan plays is the wall in *Romeo and Juliet*. This may well have become notorious since the playwright himself makes fun of a stage wall later in the Pyramus and Thisbe interlude in *A Midsummer Night's Dream*.

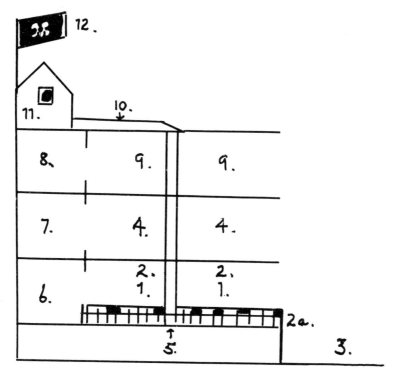

1. Apron stage
2. Audience on first tier with (2a) balustrade, partly to prevent gallant courtiers who sat at the side of the stage from falling off
3. Pit (so-called partly because the bears and bulls were let loose in this area)
4. Audience on the second tier
5. One of the columns which could represent a Roman forum, a cathedral gate, tree, mast, tent or May pole
6. Inner Below acting area
7. Inner Above acting area
8. Musicians' Gallery (also a 'heavenly' area for actors or a place to play a look-out)
9. Audience on the third tier (also known as 'the Gods' as in some theatres today)
10. Roof over the apron stage, under which a blue cloth denoted a comedy, black a tragedy
11. Manager's hut
12. The Playhouse Flag

Drawings, sketches and building contracts for the Southwark theatres on Bankside (Swan, 1596 and Globe, 1599) and the Fortune, 1600 (in what is now Barbican) have common features which these basic designs show. The large 'apron' stage had a number of trap-doors to be used for graves, tombs and the entrances of ghosts. The three levels at the back of this main acting area were curtained off—curtains making a convenient 'arras'—when not in use: with the musicians' gallery a possible area for the occasional appearance of an actor 'on high', the Inner Above for battlements or scenes in upstairs rooms, the Inner Below for interiors of churches or palaces, lawcourts, houses or inns, and the Apron for open-air scenes (woods, forest, heath or plains, gardens, battlefields, streets and public places), the Elizabethan play could move as fast as any modern 'movie'.

105

1. Apron stage

2. Audience on first tier

3. Pit

4. Audience on second tier with (4a) Stage door

5. Permanent decorated columns

6. Inner Below acting area

7. Inner Above acting area

8. Musicians' Gallery

9. Audience on third tier

10. Dashes showing the roof

11. Manager's hut

12. The flagstaff from which a trumpet would sound out 10-minute or 5-minute 'bell'

A composite drawing of a play in progress.

106

The property store—which was jointly owned by all the actors in the company—was probably below the apron stage level at the back where the actors changed and contained only the necessities mentioned in the scripts of the plays themselves. A typical inventory of any theatre's props would probably be:

2 thrones	1 chest
1 carrying litter	1 table with stools or chairs
1 bed	2 small tents

and a collection of hand-props in baskets large enough to hide a Falstaff:

Banners and flags
(heraldically correct to identify the various factions in historical or political plays)

Lanterns and flares
(to symbolise darkness, since public performances usually began at two in the afternoon)

Goblets and bottles   Maps and legal documents

Pikes, daggers, batons, staves, spades, ropes and cords

Buy a cloak, sir,   see a fair cloak,   buy a ve-ry fair cloak, sir!

Costumes were also the joint property of the company, often bought off servants who had inherited them from their masters but who were not allowed to wear 'gentlemen's' clothes. The actors wore 'modern dress' with token accessories only to mark ancient history (a Greek–Roman helmet, sash or laurel wreath) or royal precedence (crown and sceptre) worn over doublet and hose with the normal white ruff and cuffs at throat and wrists.

107

Apart from the gentlemen's 'proper habits' which also included black cloak, black hat, gloves and a sword, a company would therefore need only gowns (for lawyers, doctors, merchants, civic dignitaries *and* parsons), tabards and simple armour for the historical plays, a few 'country' costumes for shepherds, foresters and the like, old clothes for tinkers or gravediggers . . . and some women's clothes for the boys who played the female parts. The clown provided his own costume, and make-up was limited to white chalk for the faces of ghosts and murderers, with coal-black for Moors and negro slaves.

A well-known actor like Alleyn (see page 81) could afford special tailoring so that, as Tamburlaine the Great in Marlowe's play, he could be "all in scarlet" in one scene and "all in black and very melancholy" in another, but one costume usually served a character for the whole of a play, helping the audience to recognise him on sight every time he re-appeared.

All pieces of essential furniture, properties and costume changes are described as carefully as music cues in the printed texts which survive. These printed texts were made from the playwright's own, which became the prompter's copy and which was only sold to a printer in time of dire financial need or when the play dropped out of the repertory. Each actor's part was written separately by the prompter, with his own cues only, so that no one actor could sell the complete text of any company's play. Some prompt copies were stolen and pirate editions were even made from onlookers' notes, but these always lack detailed stage directions.

Printed plays were indeed as scarce as printed music.

SOURCES FOR
ELIZABETHAN DANCES

PAVAN and Galliard were the basic court dances. Both had only basic steps which matched the rhythms: 'slow, quick, quick' for the pavan and 'quick, quick, quick' in three-time for galliards. If the galliards became very brisk—and the word means a gay dance—the step could be 'slow, quick, slow, quick' with turns and improvised 'capriols' (or jumps which gave us the word 'capers'). Gentlemen who were good dancers had their own elegant variations. The pavan was a processional dance whose underlying march rhythm was carried into solemn march music by composers well into the eighteenth century. Even now, it is hard to write a march which does not move 'slow, quick, quick' unconsciously either in its tune or its underlying harmony. One particularly grave pavan was supposed to have come from Germany and was known as an Alman.

Galliards were early waltz-tunes and as they get quicker they collect syncopated accents such as the Volta on page 50. The quickest three-time music easily becomes a running exercise and the Coranto takes its name from this. What musicians call compound time—two lots of three taken together becoming 'one-two-three, two-two-three'—makes the so-called Frog Galliard on page 48 in reality a Coranto.

So to the 'long, short, long, short' rhythm of almost all country dances which not so long ago were known in England as 'rufty, tufty' dances. The Cushion Dance on page 53 clearly shows how court and country combined: when the lady dances with a partner (section A) they dance a Galliard; when she progresses with the cushion everyone goes round to a Country dance rhythm.

The only other steps were those of the Jig—a sort of jog-trot, but slightly jerky like a trotting horse—much used in Morris dancing and by comedians such as Kemp (see page 55) who 'danced' his way from London to Norwich.

Descriptions of dances in Elizabethan society are usually about their quality ("heavy", "soft", "stirring", "tumultuous" are typical adjectives) rather than formal steps, for which we have to rely almost entirely on a somewhat priggish former monk, Thoinot Arbeau, writing in 1589 about the good days he had previously known in *Orchésographie* (translated in a reprint by Dover Paperback).

SOURCES OF DRAWINGS

THE drawings are based freely on illustrations in Elizabethan books and manuscripts, tapestry and embroidery designs. The chief sources used are:

British Museum Additional Manuscript 28330   pages 31 & 65

Thomas Hill's *Profitable Art of Gardening*, 1563   47

Kemp's Nine Daies Wonder, 1600   55

A Book of Divers Devices 1585-1622   61 & 62

Two invaluable books for costume and embroidery used for details are:

The Evolution of Fashion by Margot Hamilton Hill and Peter Bucknell (Batsford 1967)
Elizabethan Embroidery by George Wingfield Digby (Faber and Faber 1970)